# *Yankee Mericana*
# MY CAPE VERDEAN ODYSSEY

by

Lena Britto

Rock Village Publishing

41 Walnut Street

Middleborough  MA  02346

(508) 946-4738

# *Yankee Mericana*
# MY CAPE VERDEAN ODYSSEY

by

Lena Britto

Rock Village Publishing

Middleborough, Massachusetts

First Printing

*Yankee Mericana*

Copyright © 2002 by Lena Britto and Edward Lodi

Typography
by Ruth Brown

ISBN 0-9674204-8-2

# DEDICATION

*to my grandparents*
*Ben and Christina Varella*

# CONTENTS

*Yankee Mericana*
# MY CAPE VERDEAN ODYSSEY

# CHAPTER ONE

# Ben Horta Varella: Whaler and Hero

I was born on April 27, 1921, on Burgess Avenue in Rochester, Massachusetts. But it wasn't until 1922 that my birth was recorded. That was because of the hardships involved in getting to the town hall. Rochester was very rural in those days and it remained so for many years.

I had a very enjoyable childhood. Mother and Dad were sweet, sweet people—poor but very loving.

I remember most of all the loving warmth of my mother. I enjoyed sitting on her lap. I was the youngest in the family and until I was about five years old, that was my special place. I would sit on my mother's lap, my hand in her bosom. I thought a mother's lap was the sweetest place a child could have to sit upon. I went around looking at laps. Fat women never impressed me. Their stomachs took up all the space. There was no room for lap. If I saw a heavyset woman who didn't have a long lap, I felt that I would never be comfortable there. I compared all other laps to my mother's. Her lap was the ideal lap.

❧

As a poor immigrant family we did not have the best of everything. We didn't even have the average of everything.

But we did have a lot of love—and made what we had look like the best of everything.

Our parents instilled in us a strong sense of family. They never let us forget the trials and tribulations they and our grandparents had in getting to this country.

My grandfather, Ben Horta Varella, was a whaler who left Cape Verde to sail on whaling ships out of New Bedford. These were the ships that sailed the world's oceans in search of whales for oil. Just a few years ago we celebrated the 110th anniversary of his first voyage to the United States, in 1886.

When the whaling industry declined he sought other work in the New Bedford area. Somehow he made his way by foot to Old Tuck in Rochester (possibly from Marion Harbor). He was away for nearly seventeen years before returning in 1903 to Cape Verde, to the city of Praia and the village of Chadã Grigoli on the island of São Tiago, to bring over his wife, Christina, and their two children.

They came to America to escape the extreme poverty of their native land. On São Tiago, where there is little rain, food was scarce and hard to obtain. Many of the people lived on plateaus on the mountains, in houses made of volcanic stone. These houses,

*Ben Varella*

which often lacked doors or windows, had roofs made of twigs. The people attempted to grow crops on the mountainside. Sometimes it would not rain for one or two years. And sometimes when it did rain, the water would wash away the seeds. (Many of these conditions still exist on the islands.)

The one thing the people did have was *esperanca*: faith; hope for the future.

As we were growing up our grandparents and mother and aunt told us of the perils they faced on the long voyage to America, of how they all came close to dying in mid Atlantic after a violent tempest ripped the mast from their vessel, the *Nauticus*. At the height of the storm my grandfather tied himself and his wife and two daughters together with a rope.

"We've been separated for seventeen years. That's long enough," he told them. "If we're going to die now, at least we'll all die together."

*Christina Varella*

Although the *Nauticus* didn't sink, it was badly damaged. It foundered for days. As they ran out of food and water the captain and crew and many of the passengers despaired. Finally, the captain committed suicide by jumping overboard. Many of the crew also gave up and were lying down to die or preparing to jump overboard like the captain.

That's when my grandfather, who was an experi-

3

enced sailor and a man of strong will, took command of the ship. He rationed out the remaining food and water and navigated the *Nauticus* until, just when they had given up all hope, they were rescued by the United States Coast Guard. When the rescue vessel appeared, Ben Horta Varella shouted out stern commands, making sure that the men allowed the women and children to board first.

A voyage that normally took thirty-five to forty days had taken more than seventy days.

My grandfather arrived on Ellis Island with his wife and two daughters and his son-in-law. My mother had recently married. She had eloped with a dapper young man from the Cabral family, who were neighbors. She eloped when she heard that her father had returned to Cape Verde to bring her, along with her mother and sister, to America.

When Ben Horta Varella found out that his daughter had married and run away with her young neighbor, Manuel Sanches Cabral, he made it known that whoever led him to them or brought them back home would be brought to America along with them.

A young man found the couple and brought them to my grandfather, and that's how my mother, who was about sixteen at the time, came to America.

My grandfather, who was born in 1851, had a good command of the English language, which he learned in his whaling days on voyages to lands as far ranging as Hawaii and California. He worked hard (he died in 1920) and saved up enough money to buy an estate called the Douglas Estate (which is still in the family) for one of his daughters, my aunt Ana.

Before going back to São Tiago, Ben Horta Varella had found employment in Rochester, initially at what became known as the Eldredge bog, then as a laborer at the Douglas Sawmill. When he returned from Cape Verde with his family, he again sought employment at the sawmill. During my grandfather's absence, Mrs. Douglas had died. Without her assistance her husband, Charles, aging and in poor health, fell upon hard times. Within a few months he sold the sawmill to my grandfather, and also found a sponsor for him. That's how Ben Horta Varella became the first Cape Verdean to settle permanently in Rochester.

*Union Cemetery*
*Rochester, Massachusetts*

He was very enterprising. Besides operating his own sawmill, he planted cranberry bogs and opened a grocery store, which his daughter Ana helped him run. He delivered groceries to the bog workers who lived in Rochester and Freetown.

He traveled by horse and buggy to help Cape Verdean immigrants when they

landed. Because they didn't know English he acted as their interpreter. He ventured as far as Providence and even Boston to

5

greet the boats and bring the immigrants to Rochester to work on the bogs.

⤷

I have not heard of very many other Cape Verdeans who came into this country by way of Ellis Island. In that, as in so many other facets of life, my grandfather was unique. In honor of his memory, and of the hardships he and his wife endured in coming to America, and in appreciation for the contributions they made to their community, in 1996 the intersection of High Street and Walnut Plain Road was named Varella Corner and a sign and an engraved stone were placed there. The inscription on the stone reads

VARELLA CORNER
Dedicated
June 29, 1996
In Memory of
Bernardino    Christina
1851 - 1920    1853 - 1932
The Long Journey from Cape Verde
Arrived 1886
*"Cu Fe Na Deus"*

The inscription says it all: "With faith in God."

⤶

6

VARELLA CORNER
DEDICATED
JUNE 29 1996
IN MEMORY OF

BERNARDINO      CHRISTINA
1851 – 1920      1853 – 1932

THE LONG JOURNEY FROM CAPE VERDE
ARRIVED 1886

EM FE NA DEUS

7

# Chapter Two

## Spelling Bee Champions

Aunt Ana was fortunate enough to attend school as a young teenager.

My mother, Matilda, was married, so she couldn't go to school. Not long after she arrived in this country she gave birth to my oldest sister, Flora Cabral Monteiro. And shortly after that my mother had a son, Theodore Cabral. She had two children

that died in infancy, and then she had the last one, Mahoney Cabral. That was the end of that family; her husband, Manuel Cabral, died a tragic death.

*Flora, with her husband Louis Santos*

*Theodore Cabral*

He was helping clear the land for a large cranberry bog (which still exists; it now belongs to the Cape Cod Cranberry Company). A huge tree fell on him and killed him instantly. He died within walking distance of his home, off of Neck Road in Rochester.

At that time my grandfather had also seen to it that his first born—my mother, Matilda—had bought a home, and that was the Stuart Estate. This property is still in the family. Members of my family and I are living here now in houses we've recently built.

My mother became a widow at an early age. Her youngest child, Mahoney, was only six months old. Flora was eleven years old, and Theodore nine.

Four years later she married Tomas Cabral Semedo, Manuel's cousin. (It was the custom for a widow, if possible, to marry a relative of her late husband. It was important that she marry someone known to be from a good family, someone of sound character, from a family line without undesirable traits such as inheritable illnesses.)

*Mahoney and Eurico*
*at house on Burgess Avenue*

Tomas was a very intelligent man. He had gone to school, had learned the English language, and was sympathetic to the plight of the young widow in Rochester who was about to lose the home purchased by her late husband. When the house, with all its land, went up for sale he was the highest bidder. As I have said, the land is in the family to this date. We hope, with God's good grace, to pass it on to our descendants for generations to come.

For convenience sake, Tomas Cabral Semedo anglicized his name to Thomas C. Smith. Not only was Smith easier to pronounce, it also sounded "more American." This was important at a time when there was often discrimination against foreigners, especially people of color (for example, in obtaining a mortgage or bank loan or taking out life insurance).

From that marriage my mother had two children: my sister Josephine and me. She also had two who were stillborn. At the time that was quite common. In the early 1900's health care wasn't what it is today.

ॐ

When I was growing up the Town of Rochester (which, as I've said, was very rural) had four district schools. The one I went to was called the Stuart School. The others were the Waterman, the Pierceville, and the Center. Even in those days they had the concept of regionalism; once or twice a year the students from all four schools got together and we had graduations and Field Days together.

The Stuart School was within walking distance of my house. The property on which it was located had been transferred to the town for one dollar. I recall my father showing us the deed, where it stated that if ever the school was demolished or done away with the property was to revert to the Smith Estate. Fortunately in time we were able to reclaim portions of it. My family and I are all located in Rochester on Burgess Avenue on the former estate of my father and mother.

*My Mother, Matilda*

*My Father, Thomas*

Even though we attended rural schools I feel that we got a great education because we learned on a one-to-one basis with our teachers. We had eight grades in the schoolhouse. Each teacher taught four grades, one through four, or five through eight. The classes were so small it was like having a private tutor.

I remember going through the first, second, third grade and it was a delight to be in school. My parents thought our schooling was the greatest thing, because they had not been educated in their country. They did everything they could to see that we went to school. My mother would often take time off from working in the garden to take a stroll through the woods to see the children at play in the school yard.

My father was Americanized because as a young man he had gone to school. (He attended night school in Worcester.) He was very active with our school and with the PTA and it made us very attentive. He was the only minority man in Rochester who attended PTA meetings. The teachers just adored him, he spoke so well.

Our teachers at that time only had to graduate from Bridgewater Normal, or whatever normal school they may have attended. But they were loving community people. They adored my father, not only because he took an interest in the PTA, but also because he helped out in many other ways. We used to sell candies to raise money to help with little incidentals the children might want, and we had whist parties, and other activities.

My sister Josephine was the spelling bee champion for the four schools for the whole town of Rochester, and I was later the champion for the fifth and sixth grades throughout the town. We received medals; the story appeared in the New Bedford *Standard-Mercury*.

Recently I looked it up. It's all on microfilm, complete with pictures of the contestants, the headline WINNERS AWAIT

CONTEST, TRIP TO WASHINGTON, and a full-page notice which included the following:

> Tuesday, April 19, 2 p.m. (Doors open at 1 p.m.) Majority of seats unreserved. Reserved section for suburban delegates and families of contestants, admission by ticket only. New Bedford Boy Scouts ushering. Music by New Bedford High School Band. Special boat schedule, arriving at 11:10 a.m., departing 5:30 p.m.

At the time, when I was eleven or twelve, it didn't interest me. But it made our parents very proud. They felt that they were the ones who were getting the education.

My sister and I went on to compete in the Greater New Bedford area. We went as far as the State Armory, where students from all over, from as far away as lower Cape Cod, competed with us. I'll never forget it: she missed on the word *menagerie*. And I missed on the word *temperature*. I left out the *a*.

Josephine, who had gone eight years to school without missing a day, came down with the whooping cough. The last day of the spelling bee, the alternate had said to her: "If you get sick, I'm the alternate, so I'll be going in your place." My mother always swore that that was my sister's downfall, because the little girl, the alternate, put a curse on her.

The whole town rallied around Josephine. They sent us books and otherwise helped out. But unfortunately because of illness she wasn't able to go to the championship match in Washington, DC.

And even if she had won, because of segregation she couldn't have gone anyhow. The year was 1932. They would not have accepted anyone of color. Likewise with the graduating class from

15

Wareham High School, they could not go to Washington because of segregation.

Growing up, we were aware of discrimination because of color. For example, black Americans were often unable to obtain life insurance. Fortunately, our John Hancock insurance man considered us Portuguese. ❧

## CHAPTER THREE

# *Hard Work and Self-Reliance*

Josephine was fortunate enough to go on to high school. I was a freshman when she graduated. I went on to my sophomore year. In the meantime, she left home to work in Boston. I was so lonely, when we received letters from her, I would say to my mother that Josephine wanted me to join her because she missed me so much. My mother couldn't read, so I interpreted my sister's letters in a way that I felt would benefit me.

I wanted so much to go to Boston! I felt, here Josephine got out of doing housework by going to work in Boston. Truthfully, I didn't see the benefit of continuing on with school. Why should I put off doing now what I'd only be doing later on? I wrangled around my mother, saying, "Josie really wants me to come to Boston," even though what my sister really had written was, "Stay in school!"

The boys, of course, had to go to work at an early age. My brother, Mahoney, helped out my sister and me a lot through school because he was able to work on the cranberry bogs until the time, at age twenty-one, when he left home to work in the steel mills out in Pennsylvania.

Pennsylvania seemed so remote, we thought he was going to the end of the world! The night before he left was a great time.

He was traveling with a few friends. They had a Model A Ford and it was a great event to see a young man leaving home. We were such a close-knit family.

He went with all of God's good wishes and prayers. It was his first time away from home and we missed him a great deal. But he provided so much for us because he saw the need, and we liked to have little things that were different, little extra things. He made sure Dad and Mother got a few dollars every week. I feel that God has blessed him time and again for what he did for our parents.

M y father never liked to work for anyone; he always preferred to be self-employed. He tried cranberry bogs. I remember him talking about building bogs, striving, farming. My parents were farm people. They made their living the best they could from the earth. That's how they were brought up in their country. Because of lack of rain there was a lot of starvation there. They considered themselves very fortunate to be in New England where we had rainfall at the times it was most needed.

A lot of immigrants from Cape Verde came to our house because my parents, and before them my grandparents, were well known in the country. They came for advice as to what they should do, whether they should work in the mills in New Bedford or stay on the cranberry bogs. Many of them stayed in the Rochester area, in West Wareham and in Tremont, in little villages near the cranberry bogs. They lived very poor lives, but to them it was rich in comparison to whence they had come. They were grateful to be able to work the bogs and the farms.

Of course, there was no Worker's Compensation or Unemployment Compensation at that time. If you got hurt on the job, that was it. You got laid off in the winter. You had to live off what you had earned in the summer, or starve. You had no recourse but to save a dollar when you could. Our parents' motto was, you made three, you saved one. They taught us to be conservative. They taught us to respect education, to get all the education we could.

We were only four Cape Verdean families that I grew up with. People of color in Rochester were few, except for the immigrants who came to work on the cranberry bogs, and they were primarily men. In that era not many women emigrated to the United States.

It was men who came to work in the factories in New Bedford or in Providence, or in construction in Boston. They didn't have unions at that time. The business owners liked the foreigners because they were hard-working, industrious people. I remember my father working in the city in the winter. He and the others were called hod-carriers. They were the ones who carried the cement for the high-rise buildings. They helped build the tall buildings that we later grew up seeing in Boston.

The Cape Verdeans did a lot of the menial work, such as the clean-up of the cement. I remember a lot of my uncles and other relatives who came from Cape Verde and settled in the Boston / Providence area to work in construction.

Dad made his home a home for all immigrants, who were always welcome. They held prayer meetings at night. They had their own ways of entertaining: string ensembles, violins, guitars, and singing at random. It was mostly church hymns that they sang, and prayers they had been taught in Portuguese or in Crioulo.

I still speak Crioulo though I got away from it after I grew up. Naturally, going to church we learned prayers in American. But at wakes that we went to with our parents, we would see the immigrants have what they called *eino*.

*Eino* was a type of mournful chanting. A group of men would sit and they would sing and chant the Hail Mary and sing the Our

*19*

Father, and most of the prayers they sang were a lament for the life of the person. It was a story that they told, encompassed in the prayers. Even at the time of my father's death, in 1947, a lot of men were still living who were able to sing *eino* at his wake.

Wakes generally lasted three days. They were held in the home, because in those days we didn't take bodies to the undertaker. It was their custom to come to the home, where they did the embalming. That's how they did it with both my grandmother and my grandfather. The undertaker did what he had to do, then brought the body to the home. The home was always used for weddings and for wakes.

People took care of the sick in their homes. I remember when my father went to the hospital. It was the biggest thing then, when he went to the hospital for appendicitis. He stayed laid up for six months. He wasn't to do a thing, just eat. My mother cooked and took care of him. Tobey Hospital, in Wareham, wasn't even built at that time. My father had to go to St. Lukes, in New Bedford, to have his appendix removed.

ᔕᐟ

My mother took in boarders, immigrants from Cape Verde, mill workers or construction workers, or people who came to work on the cranberry bogs because they could make twice as much money during the five or six weeks of harvesting season than they could elsewhere. My mother would cook meals for them. We children did the dishes, and we took care of their rooms. When the season was over, they always left us great tips. We made out almost as well as Mother did, because they all made sure we received tips for delivering milk (we had goat milk, we had cow milk) to the men who worked in the shanties belonging to the cranberry companies.

We'd rush home from school, which was practically next to

our house, to find all the tips that had been left for us. Sometimes it would amount to fifteen or twenty dollars. Believe you me, that was a lot of money for the time, when we worked for wages of only fifteen or twenty cents an hour. ᔥ

# CHAPTER FOUR

## A Strong Sense of Family

My father learned all of the music that we sang at school. He could always sing the songs we sang, and the prayers we said in English in the morning at school to start the day.

Mother never learned English, but she survived. She could count money, and she said her prayers in her own language, Crioulo. Every night she would sit and say her prayers and we would sit and pray with her, in Crioulo. As the years went by we forgot much of our native tongue. In school we had to speak English. Luckily Dad, who had some years of schooling, learned to speak the language.

When I was five years old my father worked in Worcester in construction; I couldn't wait for him to come home on weekends. He drove a big green Oldsmobile. I also remember him with an Essex and with a Packard and with Model T Fords.

He would come home with gifts for Christmas, which we celebrated at Grandma's house. (We called our grandmother "Nuggie Stina," not realizing until we were older that her actual name was Christina. "Nuggie" was the way we heard *nha*, which means "Mrs." in Crioulo.)

We were five in our family, and there were six in my Aunt Ana's family, so we were eleven altogether. We were always back and forth between each other's house, so that no one knew whose children were Maltilda's or whose were Ana's. That's the way I found it to be when I visited Cape Verde—families all bringing up their children together. Just as they did in the village of Palha Carga, that's how they did it in Rochester.

Dad worked on cranberry bogs when he came home to stay from working in Boston and Worcester. I remember him farming and picking cranberries. He built bogs right below our house. As a child I had to weed the bogs, plant vines, and pick the berries in the fall, as well as strawberries and blueberries in their season. It was hard work but it was a way to make a little extra money to help out with school clothes.

We children would pick cranberries after school. Being the youngest, I sometimes lagged behind, but I always had my chores to do. We had chickens and pigs, and we had horses and cows. We had to clean out the barn and take care of the animals. Not having any young brothers at home, my sister and I were like the little boys of the family. To help with the plowing, I rode horses bareback while my father held the plow to make the furrows.

I remember Fourth of July when we wanted to go to dances at the Roseland Ballroom in Taunton, we couldn't go until we had helped pitch in the hay. Why, we wondered, did we have to pitch hay on the Fourth? Well, that was the time of year when the hay had to be cut, when the days were sunny and hot and the hay would have a chance to dry in order to be stored in the barn, to be available for the animals in winter.

When we came home from school, my mother would be hard at work. She might be washing clothes by hand in big zinc tubs. She even made her own soap, just as they did in Cape Verde.

Mondays—wash days—we dreaded coming home from

school, because there were washtubs all over the house, and boiling water for the bleach. She used Borax to whiten the clothes. We'd have to lay the clothes out on the green grass, to bleach them—lay them on the grass and then throw on cold water, in order to make them pure white, just as they did in Cape Verde. Of course on the islands, because of lack of rainfall, there's very little grass. There the women spread the clothes on the many rocks and boulders along the coast.

I remember the times—some seventy odd years ago—when the baker used to come to deliver baked goods. In the winter he'd arrive by sled from South Middleborough. By the time he got to our house, after delivering all day in the cold, the goods that we got were frozen solid. They were hard, like crackers. But we looked forward to the raised donuts that Mother always bought, twice a week, which was how often the baker came to our house.

We would sit behind the potbellied stove in the parlor and wait to hear the sleigh bell come jingling down the unplowed country road. We'd hear the bell at night; afterward we'd put those hardtack crackers on the stove and sit behind it in our flannel nighties and wait for them to warm up. We'd heat up either cocoa or Postum and wait for the baker to arrive. He'd say to my mother, "Mrs. Smith, anything from the baker tonight?" and she'd say, "Yes. I think I like cheap cake or cookie, something like that." She meant that she would like something reasonably priced, but she would say "cheap," that's how she would say it. Of course, the baker knew exactly what she wanted. He'd go out in the cold and bring back frozen raised donuts with raisins in them. Every week, it was the same, but we always looked forward to them.

When we came home from school we'd always smell something good cooking. Sometimes it was fricassee of chicken. Oh, we were the happiest of children when a truck or car hit and killed a chicken! That meant we'd have chicken for supper. Otherwise, Mother never liked to kill her chickens because they laid eggs. The fewer the chickens, the fewer the eggs.

So, we couldn't wait to have a car hit a chicken. Sometimes we left the hen house door open on purpose, so that the chickens would wander into the road and be killed. Mother would say, "Cars are going by. Have to close the hen house door." And we'd say, "Oh yeah, Ma, it's closed." But we knew the door wasn't closed. We couldn't wait for a car to hit another chicken so that we could have chicken fricassee that night.

When we came home from school and found a big kettle on the stove, just bubbling away, we knew it was *manchupa*. Though it is one of the main dishes in Cape Verde, and popular with a lot of people, I didn't care for *manchupa*. It consisted of corn, more or less, with different meats put into it. The corn was boiled and boiled and boiled, and seasoned. It was good, but not one of my favorites.

I loved it when my mother made bread. You could smell the aroma of yeast and warm bread filling the house. There was nothing like it. I loved having fresh home-made bread with a large nickel bottle of soda.

Burgess Avenue, the street we lived on, intersected with Walnut Plain Road. If we had an extra dime or nickel, we'd cut across the field to the little country store, Isaac's, on Walnut Plain Road and spend that dime or nickel on soda or penny candy. We'd go there in the middle of the night. At least, it seemed like the middle of the night, because it was so dark. There were no street lights in Rochester. At home we just had one or two kerosene lamps burning.

We had an even bigger treat than the penny candy we bought at Isaac's Store: the fudge our older brother, Mahoney, made. When he got paid from work, he'd buy all the ingredients. Josephine and I had to be extra good, and do all the chores—make sure the wood was in, chores that he would normally do—because Mahoney was going to make fudge.

Sometimes we'd do all the chores, and he wouldn't make the fudge!

M ahoney was born in 1914. It wasn't until he was about to be married, and had to obtain his birth certificate at the Town Hall, that we found out his real name is not Mahoney, but Janeiro.

When he was still small, my mother used to take him with her whenever she went in to New Bedford to do what little shopping she did in those days. Sometimes she rode by horse and buggy from Burgess Avenue in Rochester to Mattapoisett, where she would get the trolley into New Bedford, but more often she had to walk the whole distance to Mattapoisett.

(Like all the women of her native Cape Verde, my mother wore a special cloth around her waist, to give her strength while walking. This cloth, which a girl obtained upon becoming a woman, was called a *pano de terra*. It was a prized possession, hand-made from whatever materials were available, and served many purposes: not only to give strength while walking, but also to hold a baby, or to conceal pregnancy.)

My mother would wait for the trolley at Mahoney's Hardware Store. The people who worked there asked her what the baby's name was. When she answered, "Janeiro," they said, "That's too hard to pronounce. Why don't you call him Mahoney?" So she did.

My grandmother, who couldn't pronounce Mahoney, called him "Funny."

As I'm writing this, in the year 2001, Mahoney's Hardware store in Mattapoisett (established 1884) and my brother Mahoney (established 1914) are still going strong.

We lived in a big house. It had been built by the Stuart family in the late 1800's, and had nine rooms.

Sometimes at night, as a pastime, I'd saddle Mahoney. I'd take long strings of neckties and make them into a bridle, and he was my horse. We'd go all over the house from room to room. He'd rear up like a horse and throw me off. It's hard to describe today how much fun we had. We were such a close-knit family. The love we all had for one another is something I'll treasure to the day I depart from this world.

Our biggest kick was to go to Grandma's house and play with our cousins. This is what I've tried to pass on to my own children: to be close to one another, to be loving and to enjoy the simple things of life.

Sadly, about ten years ago on a Sunday afternoon, the house on Burgess Avenue where I grew up—and where I experienced so much happiness, and shared so much love and joy, along with hardship and a lot of hard work—caught fire and burned to the ground. The cause was an overheated fireplace. But no one was hurt, a new house now stands on the property, and I have joyful memories of family and friends that no fire can ever destroy.

Moreover, my children and grandchildren live on Burgess Avenue, in houses built on property that was once part of the original estate, so that I can proudly say that we have arrived at the sixth generation. ✍

# CHAPTER FIVE

# Remembering FDR

We always had dogs. Lots of dogs.

My parents had a friend, Mr. Tinkham from Middleborough, who frequently came to visit us. He came to eat a meal and to talk. Often he'd bring a dog with him. "This is a good dog," he'd say. My parents would accept every dog he brought. I remember one named Charge, and another named Plumey. If a dog ate too much, Mr. Tinkham would bring another dog in exchange for it.

Where all those dogs came from, I have no idea.

❧

Peddlers would stop at our house. We used to buy our linoleum carpets from a man who came by in a truck. He'd carry in a carpet all rolled up, drop it onto the living room floor and lay it out.

"Three dollars."

"Too much," my mother would say. "Give you one dollar." Sometimes: "Fifty cents."

"Okay, Mrs. Smith."

Those carpets never lasted. They'd wear off in no time. There'd be nothing but black tar on the floor.

31

⋘

S am the Jew, from New Bedford, was our butcher. By the time
he got to our house it would be late in the day, and his apron,
from handling all that meat, would be dirty. Filthy. Nowadays
the government insists on inspections and whatnot. In those days
we didn't have the sanitation we have now. We never got sick,
though.

⋘

I remember the Depression years, during Hoover's term in
office, and I remember Franklin Delano Roosevelt's inauguration
in 1933. I remember going to the NRA parade in New Bedford
with Dad, Mother, Josephine, and our cousins. The parade was
in celebration of the National Recovery Act. The Depression was
over! (In our minds, at least, although the country still had a long
way to go.)

The parade was something to see, with all the floats and music
and people dancing and singing and just glad to have Roosevelt
in office. We were so thrilled to be there! Roosevelt was president
for twelve years and was about to serve another four when he
died.

His death was like the passing of a personal family friend,
the way our parents felt, so sad. We even went into mourning.
For days, we had to be quiet and speak softly and listen to the
radio. Those were sad times for all of us, because we had gone
through hard times with Hoover. We considered Roosevelt our
savior. ⋘

# CHAPTER SIX

## *Keeper of the Light*

Growing up as a child in rural Rochester, rarely did I have an opportunity to vacation in another town. It was my brother who was able to visit some of Mother and Dad's relatives. Evidently it was much easier to send a boy for a week or two: no frills, no fancy clothes to contend with (overalls would do for most occasions), no hair to comb and keep neat.

So, Mahoney got to spend school vacation in Newport, Rhode Island, where my older sister lived after she got married, or in Cohasset. Josephine and I could visit only when we tagged along with our parents to bring him home when his vacation was over.

The place that impressed us most was Cohasset, where an "uncle" of ours (actually he was my mother's first cousin) named Samuel Perry lived. He was a veteran of World War I, when Woodrow Wilson was president.

In 1917 he was stationed in France. He told us stories about his experiences during the war, what it was like to be a young Cape Verdean who spoke very little English but who survived the ordeal.

When he returned from the war he resided in Boston and married a woman named Clara. He went to night school, earned his diploma, and applied for a position as a lighthouse keeper

33

at Minot's Light.

When he was on duty he resided at the lighthouse, but off duty he lived on Hill Road in Cohasset. My family always looked forward to visiting his home which, beautifully furnished, was located on a lovely spot overlooking the ocean. From the house you could see the lighthouse far out at sea. My brother would spend part of the summer there.

Samuel Perry was an articulate person and so was his wife, Clara. They, and their beautiful home, and the lighthouse where he lived and worked, have made a lasting impression on me.

During harvesting season, which usually started the day after Labor Day, Samuel took time off from his lighthouse keeping duties to pick cranberries for the Cape Cod Cranberry Company, on the Stuart bog, located across from my present home on Burgess Avenue in Rochester. He would spend five or six weeks scooping cranberries and enjoying the fellowship of his friends.

I'll never forget the impression he made when he arrived in Rochester, driving the most beautiful car—a Buick—that we had ever seen.

⟜

At night, when everyone relaxed after supper, he would tell us of his adventures in France during World War I. I have always dreaded the rumors and the threat of war. In 1941, after Pearl Harbor, when the United States entered World War II, I recalled all those stories that Samuel had told us. I dreaded the thought of my brothers and cousins going off to war. Especially, I was afraid that they would have to endure the gas attacks that I recalled Samuel telling us about. But of course each war is different, and the Second World War had its own horrors.

⟜

S amuel Perry and his beautiful and refined wife, Clara, became our role models. They made a lasting impression on us as we were growing up.

And so, after an absence of nearly sixty-eight years, I decided to visit the area where they once lived. One day I phoned friends of mine who live in Cohasset, the O'Tooles, and asked Mrs. O'Toole if she knew where Hill Road was.

"Why, yes," she replied. "My daughter lives there."

On hearing that piece of information I became excited, and I told her about my relatives, Samuel and Clara Perry.

She said: "Well, I know my daughter lives near a Cape Verdean man, Mr. Thompson, and his wife on Hill Road."

"I don't think your daughter's neighbor is Cape Verdean," I told her.

"Oh yes," she insisted. "He's as brown as you are."

I laughed and said, "He may be my color but he is not Cape Verdean. I would have known if he was Cape Verdean by the name, not the color. Not everyone my color is Cape Verdean."

Anyhow, she gave me the Thompsons' phone number and I called them and introduced myself. When I told Mr. Thompson that my friend thought he was Cape Verdean he laughed and immediately invited me to his home. He later informed me that he is a direct descendent of the man who became the first Governor General of Jamaica when it obtained its independence from Great Britain. He himself was born in Cohasset and has lived there all his life.

Leslie Thompson has lived across the street from Samuel Perry's former residence since the age of two. He is a walking historian. He informed me that it was his father, William C. Thompson, originally from the West Indies, who built the house that Samuel lived in. And that Leslie's brother, Lancelot "Smiley" Thompson (now deceased)—who was Mahoney's playmate when

35

he visited the Perrys—played clarinet and saxophone in Billy Eckstine's band, and later for Cab Calloway and Duke Ellington.

Leslie's wife, Blanche—formerly organist at the Boston Naval Shipyard for twenty years—invited us into the music room where she graciously played the Baldwin Grand Piano, and we all ended up singing the hymn, "How Great Thou Art."

We ended the visit feeling as though we were long lost friends. The Thompsons and I plan to keep in touch. They are a delight to know, as well as a touch of history and of days gone by.

Unfortunately, back in the 1930's and '40's, I got caught up with school and other activities and Samuel Perry passed away before I as an adult could get to know him. I remember my

*Lena (on right) with Leslie and Blanche Thompson*

parents going to Boston to visit his widow. Clara and Samuel had no children.

I just had to relive that portion of my life at this late stage.

How that Hill Road has changed! Only the hill is still there. Now only in winter, when the trees are bare, can the sea be glimpsed from Samuel Perry's former home. And yet, I have found new friends on Hill Road. We are about the same age and we will try to keep in touch and visit each other, because we do not have many more tomorrows. ✍

# CHAPTER SEVEN

# Joy and Sadness

My sister went on and graduated from high school but I didn't. I quit high school in my junior year because my sister had finished school and had gone off to Boston to work, and I felt that she needed me to be with her. I felt that I could contribute more to my mother and father by being out there instead of at home.

There was no way of earning money in Rochester, so we went off to work in the homes of the wealthy in places like Newton, Brookline, and Dorchester. Working in these homes taught us a lot about life. We learned the basics; we learned about the necessities of life. I learned housekeeping, I learned about neatness, I learned homemaking skills. I learned finances. I learned a great deal in my early youth by working in the homes of the wealthy.

The people we worked for became friends of the family. They enjoyed teaching us. They were very attentive and enjoyed having the Cape Cod girls working in their homes. We would come back and recommend somebody else, and before long we had a lot of our friends from Wareham, Rochester, New Bedford and the surrounding areas taking care of children and learning housekeeping.

We were the au pairs then and we didn't have to be scrutinized. Our employers just felt that if they knew our parents (many came so far as to meet our parents), they could trust us. They saw how poor we lived and yet we were clean, we were truthful, we were industrious, and we had the initiative to be like our parents. So we had no problems getting jobs in the best of homes.

Over the years we stayed in touch. Even to this day I had friends, the Kaplans (noted philanthropists) whose home I was in when I was fifteen. Mr. Kaplan died at the age of ninety-eight. When I visited Mrs. Kaplan, shortly after her husband's death, she was in her nineties and desperate for someone to care for her. Because I was planning for my daughter's wedding and needed funds, I agreed to stay with her on a twenty-four hour basis—for seven hundred and fifty dollars a week. Seven hundred and fifty dollars a week, in a home where, as a young girl, I had scrubbed floors for four dollars a week!

When I first left home I was fourteen going on fifteen. I went to work for a Jewish doctor and his family, the Jacobs. Dr. Harvey Jacobs was at Tufts Dental School. He's the one who taught me how to iron with an electric iron, because we didn't have electricity in Rochester. I used to iron all his shirts when he was at the dental school at Tufts.

Dr. Jacobs had a brother, Leo D. Jacobs, whom my cousin Agnes worked for. They adopted us Rochester people as their family. It got so they even came to Agnes's wedding.

Of course, they only paid us four dollars a week, and I did everything. I did the cooking, the cleaning, the ironing, the washing. There were no children involved, but we did everything we could for that four dollars a week. It beat picking cranberries, it beat picking blueberries, raspberries and strawberries.

Not only did I learn housekeeping, I also learned the value of a dollar. This was the start of my ambition to become somebody.

I saw the value of education. I read a lot. We traveled in good company; you couldn't find a more intellectual group of people than those we were working for.

They were good to us. They'd say, "Do you know of any other Cape Verdean family that wants a job?" They were the people who had Morton, Stop and Shop, the Rabinovitz, the Kaplans, who as I said were great philanthropists and donated vast sums of money to hospitals. He became the national president of the NAACP. I had no regrets. They taught us well. It wasn't as if we felt inferior. It was a way of making a living and learning at the same time.

I worked for an archeologist and I summered at Martha's Vineyard. I took care of two children. The father of the children was a prisoner of war, a German married to an American. They had a home in Guatemala. They came to Cambridge to stay with her parents because he was in prison in Germany. From every home that I worked in, I learned something that I have carried with me to this day.

෴

Then the war came, and I became one of the first of the women welders. When I saw my cousins being drafted, I went with a group and took a test and passed. My brothers were married with families so they were fortunate, they didn't have to go, but I had a lot of cousins who were still single. We would go with them to the train and follow the train as they went off to their base for training. We would wave and cry and just pray that they would return and fortunately they all did.

I was a welder all during the war. I took tests for the Watertown Arsenal and ended up at the Navy Yard in Boston. I started as a 3rd class welder but soon became 1st class.

It was hard, dangerous work. We'd lie on the floor and weld

big flat pieces of steel together. I still have scars on my body from welding mishaps. Once, a welding rod went through my suede jacket and gave me a nasty burn on my left arm. Even though we wore goggles, there'd be flashes. The rays must have got through somehow. My shift was three p.m. to midnight. Sometimes, when I was home in bed, I'd wake up at two or three a.m. with a burning sensation in my eyes. Sometimes my eyes would water so badly I couldn't open them.

We welded asbestos. I sometimes wonder if working with asbestos is what eventually made my husband ill.

It was while I was a welder at the Fore River Shipyard in Quincy that I met my future husband, John Britto. He was a welder there. We got married on November 13, 1943, after a year of courtship.

Until that time I was a Roman Catholic.

John and I planned to be married at St. Patrick's in Wareham. I did all my obligations, attended all the sessions that were necessary, and seven weeks before the wedding date provided Father Callahan with the marriage license. For some reason he didn't notice that John had been previously married.

On the evening before the ceremony I went to church to

receive Communion. That's when Father Callahan told me that, because John was divorced, I couldn't be married in the Catholic Church.

"Go and live with him," he said. "But don't marry him."

*John Britto*

I couldn't believe what I was hearing. The night before my wedding, with thirty-two people in my wedding party—what was I to do? My family—my parents, my friends—would be so disappointed!

Luckily the best man—Phil Silva from Onset—knew Reverend Medina, who was a graduate of Boston University and dean of all the Protestant ministries in Wareham. He was the first ordained Cape Verdean minister in this area.

When Phil phoned him, Reverend Medina said that as long as all the necessary papers were in order we could get married the next day at St. Mark's Methodist Church on Onset Avenue. The wedding took place at 10:00 a. m. I was married to my husband for forty-three years until his death in 1986. I stayed with St. Mark's for fifty years, until I wanted to go on to a broader view of religion.

❧

During World War II gas was rationed and automobiles, which were no longer being manufactured, were scarce.

I had a car and transported a lot of women to the shipyard; they were welders, burners, timekeepers. My husband, who also had a car, carried the men. We charged the workers five dollars a week each to take them from Wareham to the shipyard. Our grocery bill at that time was five to seven dollars; things were so much cheaper than they are today. And we were making nine dollars and twelve cents a day. Eleven months after we were married we had saved up enough money to buy our own house. Talk about stretching a dollar!

We worked nights, from three to eleven. I worked seventy-two days straight without taking a day off when I thought of the boys out there fighting. I had to do my share and my husband likewise.

43

After the war I got transferred to Otis Air Force Base, where I was housemother for the young women who worked at Camp Edward. We had a lot of German soldiers who were prisoners of war, and we had a lot of young women on the base working for the government. They were stenographers, bookkeepers, the ones who took care of the business of the base. I was a dorm mother. I would watch over the young ladies to make sure there was no fraternizing with the German soldiers. I felt sorry for the prisoners, some of them were so young. They remained there until after the war, when they were shipped back to Europe.

When the war ended we had a big celebration at my house. All the workers from Camp Edwards came to our party to celebrate.

I started my family in 1947. My firstborn was Thomas. We named him after my father. It was something we both thought of at the time. My husband thought a lot of my father, and my father thought a lot of him. My father got a lot of joy having Thomas named after him.

Many years later my mother confessed: "You know, when you named your firstborn after your dad, my heart dropped." In her country, her culture, you didn't name your child after a living person.

My father was a very loving man. I'm like my father. I like people. I love to talk to people, to seek them out.

I remember the good times we had with my father.

One day he met up with someone in New Bedford who had a piano to give away. Dad was delighted to get a free piano for his daughters, Josephine and me. When the piano arrived it was the biggest piano we had ever seen. It looked like a huge mahogany casket and occupied half of a spacious living room.

44

Josephine and I played the piano and made up our own songs. Mother and Dad were just so impressed with our playing songs that we had made up ourselves! We'd also play the songs we learned in school, with Dad doing the singing.

Next we were given a Victrola, and we felt that we had reached the utmost in musical entertainment.

Dad loved the Victrola and all the new songs that came out. Once in awhile my brother would go to town with the boys and buy the latest record. We stayed up night after night. We'd wind up the Victrola and have a dance session. My sister and I were our Dad's dance partners. There was a song that went, "The music goes round and around oh oh oh." Dad would sing that and then he'd get us and we'd dance. He'd have felt boots on. Our floor, linoleum, was highly polished and slippery. It was waxed like a dance hall.

Mother never danced. She just watched. She had no sense of

music whatsoever. She was very loving, but music just wasn't her thing.

Daddy loved to sing. Josephine and I would dance with him, and then Mahoney would start. At that time there was this wildcat and Mahoney would be dancing away. My father would watch, then say, "I can do that." He

*Josephine*

45

would grab Josephine and me, and we'd dance all over the kitchen floor and into the living room.

In the wintertime Dad always had games for us to play. One game was similar to hide-and-go-seek. He'd hide a button or a spool or thread or something in the house. We had to go out of the room while he hid the object, then come back and have to find it. If we were near the object he'd say, "Warm. Warm." If we were far away he'd say, "Cold. Cold." And if we were very near he'd say, "Hot. Hot." Well, that went on and on. It was our pastime in winter.

We had another game. In Crioulo it was called *galinha branca*, which means "white hen." Dad would say, in Crioulo, something like "I gave this chicken a string of corn and that chicken went to France." Or, "the white hen went to the property of the man with the snotty nose." We children were supposed to be the chicken. He would take our hand and point his finger. Whoever he pointed to would have to leave the room. They would whisper something, and we had to find out what it was all about.

༜

My father died in 1947. He used to break in and train wild horses, which were shipped to Rochester from out West. He'd ride them bareback. Ironically it was his own horse, which he'd domesticated, which killed him. While walking the horse along Walnut Plain Road he went to swat a fly that had landed on the horse's flank. Startled, the horse kicked my father and ruptured his intestines. He died shortly afterward.

People from all over came to his funeral—friends, relatives, people he'd befriended and helped throughout the years. I remember Father Callahan turning to me and asking, "What lodge did your father belong to, to have so many people attend his funeral?" But of course he didn't belong to any lodge. People came because he was respected, and well liked.

As I've said, we were one of only four or five Cape Verdean families in Rochester. We lived more or less within a radius of one mile from each other. We all shared the same life style. None of us had electricity or running water.

We seldom got to go to the movies. I went once with my sister Flora, to see *The Crusader*. And once with the school kids to see *Little Women*.

On Sundays we would walk several miles—six miles round trip—to church in Tremont, St. Anthony's, until we were told that our parish was in Middleborough. We were happy when we had to go to the Catholic church in Middleborough because we could ride in a car, if we had one. If not, we pooled cars with our cousins and friends.

I loved books and would walk to the library, three miles to go, another three to return. We'd leave in the afternoon and return at dusk with books for evening reading and for story telling.

We always looked forward to going to school, at the Stuart School on Burgess Avenue, near our home, because that was our social life during the week. When my sister and I went on to Wareham High School, we felt as if we going to a big city.

I'll never forget the weird-looking outfit I wore my first year of high school. I sent for my clothes from Montgomery Ward with money earned from blueberry and strawberry picking. The suit cost a dollar and ninety-eight cents and the hat cost about ninety-nine cents. The suit was a two-piece cotton nubbed suit

Lena

with red and white dots. The hat was pink with an imitation leather ribbon.

The Wareham girls looked at me at the locker where I had hung my jacket. They began laughing. I thought they were laughing because my outfit was nice, but they were making a joke about my Montgomery Ward outfit that I had worked so hard to purchase. It was enough to make me leave high school my third year.

One of the girls who made fun of me, Dot Haywood, later became a close friend. Years later, when I opened my hair salon, she became a good customer. ✍

# CHAPTER EIGHT

## *Success at Many Endeavors*

My son Thomas was followed by Julius in 1949, and Vanessa in 1958. I was house-bound for a while, but I always tried to think of avenues to help my husband. When the children were young my mother was still living, and my sister was good and helped me out with Tommy. I worked for summer people on Burgess Point in Wareham. Always, in the back of my mind, I wanted to do something that would allow me to remain home with the children.

I did real estate, and then I went into factory work. I never liked working in a factory, but I tried it for a while, at night, temporarily in New Bedford making capacitors at Cornell Dublier. But it wasn't my thing.

Then I decided to go into hairdressing. After a year of schooling and tests and whatnot I passed the exam and became a registered cosmetologist. I was a hairdresser for eighteen years. I did my apprentice work in Hyannis for a year at the Hal Roux Beauty Salon. After my daughter Van was born, I would take her with me to the beauty parlor in Hyannis; we didn't have daycare or nurseries then.

In 1962 we built a large wing onto our house on Tyler Avenue in East Wareham and I opened my own beauty salon. That way I was able to earn a good living, while at the same time being home with my children.

We celebrated the grand-opening of the Van-Lee Beauty Shop with a ribbon-cutting ceremony. Selectman (later Judge) James J. Bento cut the ribbon. Afterwards, we had a reception with numerous guests. The Wareham *Courier* carried the story.

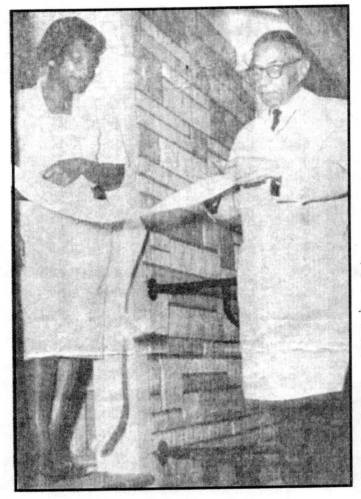

*Ribbon Cutting Ceremony for Van-Lee Beauty Shop*

*Lena with Selectman James J. Bento*

*(Courtesy of Wareham Courier)*

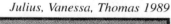

I obtained a piano and gave Van piano lessons when she was three years old to keep her busy. She loved music and went on to take piano lessons from a teacher in Marion. Later, she studied piano under the eminent pianist Henry Santos in Middleborough. She played at school in the Madrigal choir and was on the chorus team.

I gave her a lot of attention. I always involved myself in her school activities.

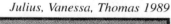

All my efforts paid off. Throughout high school the boys were active in sports, and Vanessa graduated valedictorian of her class. I remember Julius saying to me, "Mother, Vanessa has to

*Julius, Vanessa, Thomas 1989*

be able to go on to college and not work like we did to put ourselves through." I said, "I don't think you should worry. Vanessa is going to make it by scholarships." And she did. She went through Dartmouth on scholarships. And I held little events for her, flea markets or huge barbecues and whatnot. My husband and I would go to Hanover every chance we got and if he couldn't go, I'd pick up a girlfriend in Boston. We would spend time whenever a famous person was coming. We'd see the plays and the musicals that they had.

Vanessa graduated from Dartmouth with honors, then went on to Bryn Mawr. From there she went to the University of Pennsylvania, and ultimately to the University of Illinois Medical School. She is now a very successful doctor, and married to a doctor.

The boys also excelled. They loved sports. Julius obtained a graduate degree from Boston University and is now a United States Probation Officer. Tommy went into the Air Force. When he left the service he took courses and became an engineer. He now works for the MBTA as a Resident Engineer.

By following the example set by their parents, the children have all done well in their lives. We believed in hard work, we believed in honesty, in treating others as we ourselves wanted to be treated.

❧

My Dad always said to us that it's best to own your home. "Don't ever pay rent if you can help it." I used to pass this wisdom on to customers while I was doing their hair.

As I said, my husband and I bought our own house in 1943. The purchase price for that house on Tyler Avenue in East Wareham was $1500. We were able to put a down payment of $600 and obtain a mortgage for the remaining $900. I remember the amount of our first tax bill: $68.

54

Over the years, we made many additions and improvements. When I left fifty-five years later, in 1998, the house had eight rooms and a two-car garage. Needless to say, I sold it for considerably more than $1500!

My father was so proud of my home, he'd bring everyone to come and see it. Imagine! It was on a tar road and we had electricity.

My father gave us a cow, which I eventually sold, because we'd come home from the shipyard and find the cow way down there walking on Route 28.

～

I got a washing machine that went through the '44 hurricane. It was floating down Route Six near Point Road in Marion. Someone told me about it and we went down with a truck and picked it up. When we came back to East Wareham my husband, who was very mechanically-minded and could fix anything, connected it.

It was my first washing machine. I was Miss Rich. It had a ringer, and my father thought it was the best thing that could ever be. He'd bring basketfuls of clothes to wash, because they didn't have electricity in Rochester. I took in washing, and a good friend of mine, Dot Lawton, whom I'd met at the shipyard, brought over hers.

～

Meanwhile, I became a sort of entrepreneur, buying and selling real estate.

I convinced my son Julius to become a registered real estate broker. We took a course together in New Bedford. One day he didn't come in and I went by myself. The teacher asked me, "Isn't your husband coming in with you today?" Afterwards, whenever

55

I thought about what he said I laughed and laughed, thinking, "Oh my goodness, I look that young!"

Of course Julius didn't take it so lightly when I told him. "Oh," he said, "he doesn't even look at me. He doesn't see me, so how would he know how old I am?"

But anyway Julius took the course. He was only eighteen. Before he was twenty-one he passed his broker's exam, so that he became a broker without having to do practice with another firm. To this day he still has his license. I also keep mine up, because I never know when I might want to use it.

I was the first Cape Verdean woman of my generation to go into real estate. I bought up a lot of land. Unfortunately, being a woman of color, I wasn't able to develop it. Even so, I didn't lose anything. In fact I gained a lot. I learned a lot. I think of the good things that I did and have no regrets that I couldn't develop a fifty acre tract that I had in this town. A woman, especially a woman of color, attempting to develop land had too many obstacles to face in a small community like this.

Later, about the time my daughter graduated from medical school and had student loans to pay off, I received a phone call from an attorney who wanted to know whether I would sell the five acres of land I owned.

What five acres, I wondered? I had completely forgotten about them.

But to the attorney I said I'd think about it. Immediately, after hanging up, I did some research and discovered that I still owned five acres, in an area where a big development was going up. My five acres were necessary for the completion of the development. I said, "Thank you, Lord Jesus."

In the end I asked for—and received—fifty-eight thousand dollars for the land and was able to help out my daughter. So it all worked out.

I still have newspaper clippings recounting my exploits as a real estate agent:

"Century 21 has added Lena S. Britto to its sales staff. A real estate veteran, Britto brings to the firm over twenty years experience in residential real estate and land in the Wareham and Rochester area." Another clipping reads: "Achievement awards for November were presented to associates of the Jack Conway Company's Wareham office. Lena Britto of Tyler Avenue, East Wareham, negotiated the most sales."

I was invited to become a member of the Board for the Sandwich Co-operative Bank. When I received the invitation I was flabbergasted. "If you want me, I'll be glad to serve," I said.

At first, when I went to the meeting, everyone looked at me as if I didn't belong. But they soon got to know me!

When my husband retired in the 60's I felt, "Oh my goodness, I've got to get a really well-paying job, something with health insurance." That's when I went to work for the New England Farm Workers Council, and later, the Department of Social Services.

I love helping children. I love steering children in the right direction.

Even though I'm now eighty years old, young people seem to want to be in my company. One reason is that I think young. And I've never lost my sense of humor. Or my compassion for others.

57

I remember counseling a young woman, a rape victim. She had been raped at the age of five. "You're a stronger woman for going through what you went through," I told her. "Don't let it be a problem. Use your experience as a basis to reach out and help others."

I do a lot of volunteer work. I believe in the adage, "What you sow is what you reap." That was true with my parents, likewise with me and my children. Life is what you put into it. If you do the right thing, it will come back to you many times in great folds. ◅

# CHAPTER NINE

## *Mothers and Daughters*

My mother was a sweet, warm, loving mother, very caring. Some days she would sit in the kitchen and look longingly out the window. She would begin to hum and sing, and soon tears would be rolling down her eyes.

I'd say, "Ma, what's wrong? Why are you crying?"

"Oh my dear, you don't know anything about life."

She was lamenting the past, thinking about the youngsters, the girlfriends she'd left behind in Cape Verde, and wondering about the poverty they had to endure. Here she was, living in a much richer country which most of them would never see. Regardless of the fact that in America we, too, were poor, our poverty was far different from the real poverty that she came from.

I'd say, "Well, Mom, there's nothing you can do about it."

She'd turn to me and say, "Dear child, you don't realize. Some day you'll know what love for your home, love for your family and friends that you left behind, is all about."

❧

She would tell us, "Always leave the door open for Mother." If looking down the road she saw Gramma coming to visit (they lived about a mile apart), she'd open the door and leave it open, even when Gramma was still far down the line.

I'd ask, "Ma, why do you want to open the door? She's almost five minutes away."

"You always open the door for your mother. When you see your mother coming towards your house, that door should always be open." She'd also say, "Mother is like a very tender piece of meat, with not a piece of bone on it. She is all love with no malice or selfishness in her."

And that's the type of mother I tried to be.

When I had my hairdressing business in my home I set aside Mondays as my day off. Beginning when my daughter was not yet in school, I referred to Monday as "our day off." I always included Vanessa in any plans I had for the day. We would generally go to Boston and visit the State House or the Prudential Building or our elected officials.

One day I told Vanessa and her girlfriend that on the following Monday we would go and meet Governor Volpe. Van told all the customers that came into the shop that we were going to visit the governor.

The customers just said, "Really?" or asked, "Why?"

"Mother said we are going to visit our governor. I'm going to be a lawyer when I grow up," was her answer.

We did get to visit the governor, and he was so impressed that I had brought my daughter and her friend to meet him that he called for the photographer, and had a picture taken of us with him in his office.

*Lena, Vanessa and friend with Governor Volpe*

# CHAPTER TEN

# *A Little Girl Lost*

In 1947 a small child from the nearby town of Plympton strayed from her home and became lost in the Carver woods. Irma Santos was only five years old; she wandered for two days before she was found in a swamp near some cranberry bogs. It was winter. The temperature at night had dropped to almost zero. Irma was taken to Massachusetts General Hospital in Boston. Her feet, badly frost-bitten, had to be amputated.

Besides having to endure a great deal of pain, little Irma was faced with the prospect of needing artificial feet for the rest of her life. In those days, of course, there was no television, but her plight had been mentioned in all the newspapers and on the radio.

One day when I was feeding my baby, Tommy, and listening to the radio I heard the pianist Hazel Scott being interviewed at Symphony Hall in Boston. The thought came to me: if only I could persuade this world-famous woman to come to Wareham and give a concert to benefit the little girl from Plympton who lost both feet from frost bite!

Immediately, I phoned the radio station and spoke to Hazel Scott's press agent. He listened to the sad story of the five-year-old child languishing at Mass. General and agreed to talk to Miss Scott and call me back. The next day he did call me back, from

New York, with the wonderful news that Hazel Scott would gladly give a concert in Wareham to benefit little Irma.

There were, however, certain conditions to be met, several strict rules that we (I and my fellow Sewing Circle club members, whom I'd ask to assist me) had to follow.

We had to provide a hall for the concert that could accommodate at least five hundred people.

We had to provide a Baldwin Grand Piano. No other piano would do.

We had to provide the best of cars for Miss Scott and her entourage to ride in.

We had to meet Miss Scott at the train station and provide her with a police escort all the way from Boston to Wareham.

"I can do all that," I assured the press agent.

*How can I ever do all that?* I asked myself after we'd finished talking. *What have I got myself into?*

ക

Suddenly, I found myself personally responsible for bringing—in style—an internationally known classical and jazz pianist to the small town of Wareham, Massachusetts.

For those younger readers who may not remember Hazel Scott, I'll take the time now to include just a few of the details of her life, some of which I remember, others of which I have researched for this book.

Hazel Scott was born in Trinidad in 1920 (about a year before I was born in Rochester) but came with her family in 1924 to live in Harlem. From an early age she showed musical talent. She trained at the Juilliard School of Music and was still a teenager when she made her Broadway debut. Soon after that she played at Carnegie Hall. She continued to perform on Broadway and went on to appear in a number of Hollywood films, such as

*Something to Shout About* and *Rhapsody in Blue*. She could play both classical music and swing music. In later years she appeared on television, in series such as *Julia* and *Playhouse 90*.

Hazel Scott was a woman who was proud of her African heritage, and very active in civil rights. She absolutely refused to perform before segregated audiences. In 1945 she married Adam Clayton Powell, Jr., an influential United States Congressman from New York.

*Hazel Scott and Irma at Mass. General Hospital*

The wife of Adam Clayton Powell, Jr., had to ride in the best of cars and with a police escort.

⁊

After the phone conversation with the press agent, I got busy with my committee of Sewing Circle friends and within a few days we found two late model Buicks within my family. One belonged to my cousin Manuel Tavares, and the other to my cousin Arthur Tavares.

Someone mentioned that Dr. Stillman, a prominent doctor in Wareham, owned a Baldwin Grand Piano. Dr. Stillman graciously made it available for the concert, which would be held at the Wareham Town Hall.

In the meantime, the press agent contacted the Massachusetts State Police and arranged for a police escort for Congressman Adam Clayton Powell's wife from the train station to Mass. General Hospital, and from there to the Town Hall in Wareham. Governor Bradford was the governor of Massachusetts at that time. He saw to it that Miss Scott was afforded all the honor and protection the Commonwealth could offer.

⁊

The day of the concert I greeted Hazel Scott at the Back Bay Station in Boston. I was so impressed and excited and overwhelmed with all that was happening when she appeared before me dressed ready to go on stage to perform! I couldn't believe what was unfolding before my eyes. Here was this beautiful woman wrapped in one of the rarest of mink coats in the world, so elegantly poised.

I thought I must be dreaming.

We were rushed into the waiting cars and escorted by the Boston City Police to Mass. General, where Miss Scott met the brave little child for whose benefit she was to perform, and presented her own personal check to her. Then we were escorted to where Route 28, the State Highway, began in Mattapan.

There, all the State Police with their Captain were lined up on both sides of the highway waiting for our entourage, to lead us in a motorcade to the Town Hall in Wareham. It was a beautiful sight to see all the officers in their blue uniforms, the same color as their blue cars.

I sat with Hazel Scott in the back seat of one of the Buicks and her press agent sat in front, beside the driver. The Captain gave instructions to the drivers and asked, "Can you keep up with us? We do not stop for red lights and we do not drive under sixty-five miles per hour. Can you handle it?"

My cousin, Manuel, said: "I think so."

The Captain said: "If you can't handle it, say so now." This was the old Route 28, before they built the modern highways. It was a dangerous road, all full of curves; there were fifty miles of it between where we started from and the Town Hall in Wareham. And these were the days before seat belts or air bags had even been thought of.

Manuel looked up at the Captain and grinned. "I can handle it. You don't know how many times I've left you behind."

The Captain and the others who heard all laughed.

ॐ

I had never before been in a car driven under police escort. I tried to start a conversation with Hazel Scott. We talked about our children. Her son, Adam Clayton Powell III, was the same age as my son, six months. I tried so hard to enjoy her and there was so much that I would like to have said. But speeding along at sixty-five or seventy miles an hour around curves and through red lights, I was just not able to relax.

I was so petrified, I prayed all the way.

ↂ

We arrived in Wareham in good time. The selectmen had made sure that the Wareham police were on hand. The Town Hall parking lot was full, and there were cars lining Route 6 all the way down the hill and along Main Street to the center of town. Even in the parking lot of the First National, not an empty space was to be found. Late arrivals had to park along Route 6 heading toward Marion.

Everyone who could be there, was there. We had a full house. The Town Hall was packed to capacity.

Dr. Goldfarb, our family doctor, made the opening remarks to welcome the guests that evening and stated the purpose of the concert. Then the press agent spoke and asked everyone to donate generously because in the coming years little Irma Santos would need all the help she could get.

Miss Scott played classical music and was well received. From that concert and other donations from surrounding towns, and from all over, we were able to raise enough money to take care of Irma's medical needs until she turned twenty-one. Believe me, it was a great feeling, to think that a group of women could get together and organize to help a child in need.

Even after more than half a century I still see Irma, who has children of her own and grandchildren. She always talks about how grateful she is and thanks us for the help we extended to her.

ↂ

I remember that the first person who greeted us at the Town Hall that night was my Dad. He was so proud that my friends and I had done such a wonderful deed.

That was the year that he passed away. ↜

68

# CHAPTER ELEVEN

# My Years as a Social Worker

After my husband retired I went into social work, first for the New England Farm Workers Council, and then for the Commonwealth of Massachusetts Department of Social Services.

Many of the farm workers I came into contact with were Puerto Ricans who spoke only Spanish. Because Spanish is similar to Portuguese, I could understand the workers' needs and help them solve their problems.

The needs of the workers were many. They had come to the New England area to work seasonally, on cranberry bogs or on large vegetable farms. Often they lived in substandard housing. Sometimes their needs were basic, such as warm blankets for the cold nights in the fall during harvesting. If they needed counseling in the court system we were there for them. Some were illiterate. I enrolled several in night school so that they could learn to read and write English.

Our church, St. Mark's Methodist Church, on Onset Avenue, under the leadership of the late Reverend Frederico Medina (our minister for forty years) was very supportive, helping the workers spiritually, socially, and materially.

After two and one-half years with the New England Farm Workers, I went to work for the Department of Social Services, at the New Bedford and Brockton offices.

I was responsible for placing children in foster homes and visiting them as often as necessary. I would travel many miles to visit children placed in Catholic homes as far away as Marlboro. I tried to be very faithful with these visits because I was always concerned about the children, as if they were my very own.

After ten years, I retired from the Department of Social Services. But while I was still employed, the state offered social workers an opportunity to complete their education. I decided to go for my BA degree.

Not having finished high school, I felt somehow short-changed. At meetings my co-workers would mention their backgrounds, their years of college, their degrees. I had only two or three years of high school, and no degree.

I discussed the matter with my family. My daughter was in college in Illinois; I felt that I could not afford to pay for both her expenses and mine. Then I was offered free tuition to attend the University of Massachusetts. I was delighted! I worked hard to make sure that I graduated from college the year before my daughter—I didn't want to interfere with her graduation year.

My classes were held in Boston.

On school days I would get out of work early, around three o'clock. I'd take the bus from Wareham into Boston, and wouldn't get back to Wareham until well past midnight. I'd drive in the dark and arrive home in darkness. My husband would be fast asleep. And then I'd have to repeat the whole process again the next day.

Today, whenever I see a Bonanza bus I get an upset stomach, thinking of the exhausting schedule I maintained! I was sixty-four years old when I got my bachelor's degree.

70

*Graduation Day*

While my family was taking pictures at the graduation ceremony someone asked my son, Julius: "Is that your daughter?"

He went into a tizzy. "No, that's my mother!"

"Oh, Julius," I said, "I could be your daughter."

"He's just trying to make you feel good," Julius said.

But I know Julius was proud of me, just the same.

☙

I told my children, I want a graduation party just like each of you had when you graduated from high school. I was determined: I was not going to take my cap and gown off all day. Luckily it was May 30th, and the weather was cool. But even if it had been a hundred degrees outside I still would not have taken off the cap and gown that I had worked so hard for.

My good friend Belmira Nunes, the well known educator and writer—who, in 1917, was valedictorian of her class in Warehm High School—came all the way from Florida to attend my graduation and party. In her youth, when racism was very prevalent, she had experienced discrimination, such as not being allowed to travel with her class to Washington, DC—despite the fact that she was class valedictorian. ❧

# CHAPTER TWELVE

## *My Equestrian Adventure*

One year my husband and I decided to get horses for our children.

The boys were going through horseback-riding stages, so one day John took them horse hunting and returned with a lovely horse a friend of his had recommended. We owned a barn—already there when, years ago, we bought the house in East Wareham—as well as an open space consisting of a couple of acres of splendid farmland.

Vanessa was growing, so her dad decided she could have a smaller horse for her own. She quickly learned to ride and did very well.

Eventually my eldest son, Thomas, went into the Air Force; Julius now had full possession of the horse and would ride occasionally.

❦

One year Tommy sent home a saddle from Panama as a gift for Mother's Day. It was a truly beautiful saddle and I was very pleased. So I told my daughter that I would like to ride all the way to Rochester from East Wareham.

On a pleasant Sunday afternoon we began our ride.

Beforehand, I phoned the Wareham police and asked them to please be aware that my daughter and I would be riding through town on our horses. I was particularly concerned that when we crossed the Narrows Bridge the horses might shy and be a hazard to us and to traffic. But when we arrived at the Narrows the police were there and all went well.

We then proceeded through town along Merchants Way near the railroad track, onto Main Street to Lincoln Hill and Fearing Hill Road, then on to Rochester. We had it all mapped out.

I had on a strikingly beautiful riding jacket. And being a professional hairdresser and wishing to be fashionable I decided that I would add to my image as a glamorous horsewoman with a beautiful hairdo. I would at the same time be advertising my profession.

We galloped slowly along County Road and turned onto High Street. All along the way, as we passed the houses of people who knew us they waved, then relayed the message ahead that Lena and Vanessa were traveling on horseback from East Wareham to Rochester.

In Rochester my brother was hosting an annual picnic at his grove. The guests included three busloads of people from Boston. It was my intention to make a grand entrance on horseback as a Cape Cod lady and her daughter. How I would impress them as a fashionable equestrienne, with my brand-new saddle, beautiful jacket, and fancy hairdo!

At this point Vanessa decided that we had trotted long enough, so she spurred her horse, which took off like a bullet. Seeing this, my horse suddenly broke into a gallop in order to catch up.

My horse flew along so quickly that I couldn't control it. To hold her back I grabbed onto the reins with both hands. As I did so my "hairdo" flew off my head onto the road. I left it far behind in the dust as I made my "grand" entrance into the grove with no

74

wig and looking like a wild woman who had just been up to something totally lacking class.

My son, home from the service, was at the picnic grove and saw my predicament. He ran down the road and retrieved my wig. It was covered with sand, and I put it on backwards. I was so embarrassed, after that I never again wore a wig.

That was the most embarrassing moment of my life! ﾃ

# CHAPTER THIRTEEN

# *Amilcar Lopes Cabral, Liberator*

In 1975 Cape Verde obtained its independence from Portugal. This occurred only after a long armed struggle—fought primarily in the Portuguese colony of Guinea—and largely through the heroic efforts of Amílcar Lopes Cabral, one of the founders of the PAIGC (*Partido Africano da Independéncia de Guinea e Cabo Verde*)—the African Party for the Independence of Guinea and the Cape Verde Islands.

❧

The first time I heard of Amílcar Cabral was on the radio. He was being interviewed in North Carolina, where he was studying agriculture: in particular, irrigation methods and what could possibly be done to produce more food for drought-stricken *Cabo Verde*. From the radio I was able to get his home address in Conakry, Africa.

When he returned to Africa I wrote to him and explained that we were his family, that my parents were Cabrals from his village in *Cabo Verde* who immigrated to the United States in the early 1900's.

He received my letter and was delighted to hear from the American relatives that he had been told about when he was growing up.

Although Amílcar Lopes Cabral—considered the father of African nationalism in the former Portuguese colonies of the Cape Verde Islands and Guinea-Bissau—was born (on September 12, 1924) in Bafatá, Guinea, his father, Juvenal António da Costa Cabral, was born on the island of São Tiago, Cape Verde, the island of my ancestors. Amílcar's mother, Iva Pinhal Evora, also was born on São Tiago. From the age of seven, Amílcar attended school in Cape Verde before going on in 1945 to study in Lisbon.

Throughout these years he wrote poetry, stories, and plays. He was deeply affected by the suffering and the poverty of the Cape Verdean people. In the years he lived there he witnessed a drought that lasted eight years. More than 50,000 people, almost a third of the population, died from starvation and deprivation during that time.

NESTA CASA VIVEU

AMILCAR CABRAL

PARTE DA SUA INFÂNCIA

In 1956 he and five others founded the PAIGC. This is the party that began the struggle for independence. The guerrilla war against the Portuguese, waged mostly in Guinea, began in 1962 and didn't end until 1973. Besides being the most important political leader, Amílcar also served the cause through his writings and his diplomatic efforts.

In 1973, Amílcar Lopes Cabral was assassinated in Conakry, the capital of Guinée (a former French colony).

Approximately three weeks before he was assassinated he received the letter that I had written to him. Although he was able to write a letter in response, he did not have a chance to mail it before he was gunned down.

The letter that he wrote to me but never sent is now at the Amílcar Cabral Foundation in Cape Verde. In 1988 I obtained a

*Childhood home of Amílcar Cabral*

copy of the letter from Ana Maria Cabral, Amílcar's widow (who as a young woman fought at his side in Guinea).

✍

In the chapter that follows I've included transcripts of both letters—the one I sent to Amílcar Cabral, and the one which he wrote in response, but never mailed.

(The expression *Nha Pincha*, which I used as the closing of my letter, means "Let's push.") ✍

## CHAPTER FOURTEEN

# A Tragic Correspondence

Following is a transcript of the letter that I sent to Amílcar Cabral in 1973, just three weeks before he was assassinated:

Dear Amílcar Cabral,

I know you will be surprised to get this letter. I am an American Cape Verdean born of Cape Verdean parentage. My people are also Cabrals who emigrated to this country in 1875 and 1900's. I feel that we are related. My grandfather, who first came in 1875, went back to Cape Verde and brought back his wife and two daughters. My grandfather was Ben Varella. My grandmother was Christina Morriera from Praia. They settled in Massachusetts on Cape Cod. I have met Gil Fernandes and enjoyed everything he had to say. Also a young man by the name of Sala Mathews, originally from my town.

I wish I knew you were in America. I would have made an effort to have contacted you. I am sure that we are your cousins. I have read a book about your work and I certainly do admire what you are doing. May God bless.

I have three children and my husband joins me in

wishing you well.

I have every intention of visiting Cape Verde in the very near future.

If you should come to America please call or write to me. Hope we do meet. I'll pray. As we were told *Nha Pincha*.

Yours Sincerely,

Mrs. John (Lena) Britto
17 Tyler Ave.
East Wareham, Mass. 02538

P.S.
Answer as soon as you receive this. Then I will know that there is a possibility of communication.

ھ

Following is a transcript of the rough draft of the letter that Amílcar Cabral wrote in reply to the letter he received from me, but which he did not live long enough to mail:

Dear Mrs. Britto,

I've just received your very kind letter, and I thank you very much and your husband for your attention.

I also do feel we are cousins, because my family is also from São Tiago. In any case we can do it true— and from now on we are surely cousins.

I hope we can meet as soon as possible. Soon, another colleague of mine will travel to the States and I'll send him to you. Happy New Year for my family I will know.

Yours Sincerely,
Amílcar

82

Dear Amilcar Cabral,

I know you will be surprise to get this letter. I am an American Cape Verdean born of Cape Verdean parentage. My people are also Cabrals who migrated to this Country in 1875 and 900's. I feel that we are related. My grandfather first came in 1845 went back to Cape Verde and brought back his wife and two daughters. My grandfather was Ben Varrella my Grandmother was Christina Moreira from ~~Praia~~ Praia They settled in Massachusetts or Cape Cod. I have met Gil Fernandes and enjoyed everything he had to say also a Young man by the name of Sola Matthews originally from my town

I wished I knew you were in America, I would have made an effort to have contacted you. I am sure that we are your cousins. I have read a book about your work and I certainly do admire what you are doing. May God Bless.

83

I have three children and my
husband joins me in wishing you well.
I have every intentions of visiting
Cape Verde in the very near future.
If you should come to America
please call or write to me. Hope we
do meet. I'll pray. As we were
told "Mi Pinche."

Yours Sincerely,
Mrs John Britto
17 Tyler Ave. East Wareha
Mass
02538

P.S.
Answer as soon as you receive this
then I will know that there is a possibili
of communication.

Dear Mrs. Britt.

I've just received your very kind letter, and I thank you very much and your husband for your attention.

I also do feel we are cousins, because my family is also from S. Tiago. In any case we can do it true — and from now we are surely cousins. ~~...~~

I hope we can meet as soon as possible. Soon, an other colleague of mine will travel to the States and I send him to see you. Happy New Year for all my family I will know.

Yours sincerely,
Andre —

85

## CHAPTER FIFTEEN

# ℒike a 𝒥ourney ℋome

In the 1970's I had been quite active in supporting the struggle for the liberation of *Cabo Verde* from Portugal and had joined several organizations in this country. My son, Julius, was also very active and was one of several Americans who rode triumphantly with the new government from Sal into Praia in 1975. (The New York *Times* ran an article that referred to Julius as "the bearded American.")

In 1984 my husband, John, and I made our first trip to Cape Verde.

Knowing that I can be outspoken, people said to me, "Be careful what you say there."

I said: "I'm going as a free black woman born in America. I'll say what I have to say, so long as it's the truth. If they put me in jail, I'll get out, eventually."

But as it turned out, I had nothing but a wonderful time.

We traveled via Dakar, the capital of Senegal on the western coast of Africa. We left New York at midnight on February

6th and arrived in Dakar ten o'clock the next morning. Although it was February, the heat was intense. We visited several places but could not understand the language at all. Luckily there was a large colony of Cape Verdeans, who helped us to board the plane to *Cabo Verde*.

We arrived in Cape Verde at three p.m. after a three hour flight. We settled into the Hotel Praia Mar. It was then that I really relaxed and felt at home. We had always kept in touch with my parents' people. But here I was, the first generation of my mother and father's American family to actually come back and check out our roots.

We had written in advance to inform our Cape Verdean relatives of the day of our arrival. The first morning when I woke up and looked out the verandah door I saw a young man standing below, peering up at our window, as if to catch a glimpse of his American relatives. He looked exactly like my oldest son, Tommy! Even a stranger could have seen the family resemblance.

I called to him and invited him up to our room. I wept when he told me he was the grandson of my first cousin, my father's niece. She had died several years prior to my arrival, but I knew all about her. We had exchanged letters, and as was the custom of my parents I had sent clothes and financial help.

We spent a month in Cape Verde. We traveled with family, who took us to meet other family members in Palha Carga, the village of my ancestors. We spent a night in one of the homes in the mountains—the home of my mother's niece, Johana, who has since passed away. At the time, she was the oldest living member of our family in *Cabo Verde*.

I made a second trip in 1986 to attend a wedding. My husband had passed away; I was accompanied by eight women. Since

I was a widow, a young nephew of my father's named Eurico offered to come and stay with me in America. I approached the officials, and after a couple of years I went back to Cape Verde, and he was able to return with me to the United States. He was the first of my father's people that I was able to bring here to America. Since then, he has brought over his mother and brother and others, to enjoy all the good things with which God has blessed the good old USA.

⁂

All told, I've made six trips to Cape Verde. On one of these I served as tour guide and interpreter for seventeen women, most of whom were first generation Cape Verdeans born in America. The reason I was chosen spokesperson was my fluency in *Crioulo*, which I learned to speak perfectly at home growing up in Rochester with my parents and siblings and cousins and friends. ⸙

*Cara Mount, Rubon Manuel*

# CHAPTER SIXTEEN

# *Rubon Manuel*

I could not look back on my life without writing about my grandfather, Ben Horta Varella's, home town in *Cabo Verde*.

For my 80th birthday my children and grandchildren took me out to a fine restaurant in Rhode Island. After lavishing upon me all sorts of beautiful tributes, they surprised me with a round trip ticket to Cape Verde, and the opportunity to visit Rubon Manuel, the town Ben Horta Varella left behind when he was twenty-three years old.

❧

We left home for New York on July 10, 2001. This was my sixth trip to West Africa and *Cabo Verde*. I had with me my daughter and her husband, who are both doctors, so I felt very secure traveling out of the country at my age.

When I arrived at the hotel I discovered that word had gotten out that "Donna Lena," the "Mericana Britto," had once again come to *Cabo Verde*. Over the years I have befriended so many people that I was inundated with visitors—men, women, and children from all over the island. My hotel seemed like Grand Central Station. Truly I felt—as I have felt for many years—that I am an ambassador of good will from America.

M y two granddaughters joined us the second week in *Cabo Verde*. We were at the airport to meet them. The view of the Atlantic Ocean and the plane landing in Praia was just breathtaking—much improved since I was there in 1989.

What excitement to see the expressions on the faces of the fifth generation upon seeing for the first time the homeland of their great great grandparents!

*Landing at Praia*

O n August 13, 2001—more than one hundred years after my grandfather's departure—I arrived at Rubon Manuel. We had an eight-passenger van and a very good driver who, for the equivalent of eleven US dollars a day, drove us to Palha Carga where my family was located and on to Rubon Manuel.

The roads to the village, unpaved and pocked with deep holes, consist mostly of sand and volcanic stone—nothing like the roads we have here in America. The terrain is mountainous, the land parched (there is no rainy season and sometimes no rain for years at a time) with no greenery whatsoever. No trees, no grass, no beautiful scenery, just steep hills and deep valleys and hairpin curves. And very few horses, mostly just donkeys to carry water and twigs for burning. To get from one place to another the people have to walk.

The journey of one and one-half hours (we made the trip three times!) was so perilous that more than once I felt like asking the driver to turn around and head back to the hotel. Mile after mile we ascended and descended along roads carved into the hillsides, the driver all the while tooting his horn to warn any cars that might be approaching around the bend. As we rounded each blind curve I prayed that we would not plunge over the edge of the mountain or crash head-on into another vehicle.

ॐ

In such a land famine is a constant concern. Most of the people depend on farms to survive—provided it rains, and that is rare.

ॐ

The people depend a great deal on donkeys.

The donkeys make many trips each day to the water holes. Their owners strap plastic containers across the backs of the  animals and send them to the river to fetch the water at the foot of the mountain, where someone is always waiting to fill the containers and tie them to the donkeys' saddle and send them back up the mountain. We continually met several donkeys going to and fro,

93

working as busily as any human beings.

It was fascinating to watch them go about performing their duties of delivering water to their owners, or carrying bundles of twigs up from the valleys for fuel for cooking. Donkeys are cheaper to feed than horses, and because of their smaller size they are more easily handled by children.

✍

There is an interesting episode from history connected with Rubon Manuel.

But it was only after considerable coaxing that I was able to pry the story from my friends and relatives in Palha Carga, who consider the subject somewhat indelicate. When I informed them of my desire to visit the area, they tried to dissuade me.

"You don't want to go there," they insisted. "The women there are rough."

✍

The incident occurred in the time of Sir Francis Drake when England was attempting to take control of Cape Verde from Portugal. When the women heard that the English were coming on horses to capture the men of Rubon Manuel in order to sell them into slavery, they took charge and sent the men into hiding in the surrounding mountains, where the English could not follow on horseback.

As the English cavalry entered the village the women assumed the role of warriors and attacked and fought them. They knocked the cavalrymen from their horses, pinned them to the ground by sitting on them, and urinated in their faces! After that, the English scrambled back onto their horses and galloped away.

Imagine the embarrassment of the men when they returned from the mountains and learned that the women had taken charge and beaten back the enemy!

ॐ

When the English attacked, the women were picking a type of bean called *porginha*. The oil from this valuable bean

*Porginha*

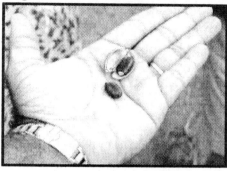

has many uses: as an antiseptic and for lamp oil. The people also use it as a bath oil and for rubbing on dry skin. The women use it during pregnancy. As with so many herbs in *Cabo Verde*, it serves a number of medicinal purposes.

ॐ

It is the people themselves who make Cape Verde so special. I can never forget the emotions displayed by the elderly, the hospitality extended, the expressions on the faces of the children. In the village men and women cried to think that their family from America had come all that way, across the sea and over the mountains, just to meet them.

*Lena , with cousins in Cape Verde*

*Cannons at Cidade Valha*

*Oldest tree in the world (Benventura, Cape Verde)*

# CHAPTER SEVENTEEN

## *Ana Maria Cabral, First Lady of Cabo Verde*

During my visit to Cape Verde in 1988 I fervently hoped to meet Ana Maria Cabral, Amílcar's widow—who had fought by his side in the fight for independence. On this trip I was accompanied by my daughter, Vanessa. We made inquiries and were told about the Amílcar Cabral Foundation.

We visited the foundation, where we met the most gracious, pleasant, beautiful woman in all of Cape Verde, who ushered us into her office. I was so excited that I wept. I had often thought about meeting Ana Maria someday, just as long ago— before fate cruelly intervened— it had been my most heartfelt desire to meet Amílcar Cabral personally.

We sat and looked at each other and I told her about the letter I had written to her

*Lena meeting Ana Maria*

husband three weeks before his assassination.

She started to cry and said, "Yes, I have the letter you wrote. And he did answer with a letter of his own, which he didn't live to mail." Then she reached into her desk and there—amongst all the letters from all over the world that she had received—she pulled out the one that I had sent to him just three weeks before his death.

I remembered when, years before, I heard on the radio that the man I so much admired, and so much desired to meet, had

been viciously murdered. At that moment, deep in my heart, I had given in to despair and felt that life wasn't worth living. When I phoned my son in California and informed him of the assassination, he wept.

૭

The airport in Sal is named for the Liberator, Amílcar Cabral, and a beautiful statue has been erected in his honor.

૭

I invited Ana Maria Cabral to America to help celebrate Wareham's 250th anniversary. The Cape Verdean government sent her to stay with my family for one month. (The president of *Cabo*

*Statue of Amílcar Cabral,*
*Sal International Airport*

*Verde*, Aristides Rievera, greatly encouraged her to make the trip. My husband and I visited the president in 1984 in Cape Verde, and I attended his reception in Governor Dukakis's office in Massachusetts when he himself visited this country.)

Together Ana Maria and I visited many places in America, including the Cape Verdean consulate in New York and the embassy in Washington. We also visited Lincoln University, where Amílcar had studied while in the United States.

ço

When I first met Ana Maria in *Cabo Verde* I secretly pictured her coming some day to America, where the two of us would sit on my bed and talk, like two sisters.

And that's exactly how it turned out. When she visited me in Wareham we sat on the bed and I asked, "What happened?" I was referring to the assassination. "Tell me, how did it happen?"

And she told me. They had gone out to dinner, then returned home. He was surrounded by his body guards. It was his own guards, that the Portuguese government had bribed, who shot him. ✒

*Ana Maria Cabral*

# Reflections

I have no regrets for whatever hardships or minor disappointments I may have encountered in my life. All my life experiences were challenges that, with faith in God, I was always able to overcome.

I have always tried to be supportive of my children's dreams and ambitions, and I am very grateful for all their many achievements. ✐

# GLOSSARY
of *Crioulo* Words and Phrases

*eino*: a type of mournful, chanting prayer; a lament for a deceased person

*esperanca*: faith; hope for the future

*galinha branca*: (literally, white hen); a type of children's or parlor game

*manchupa*: a seasoned dish consisting of boiled corn and meat

*nha*: (term of respect for a woman held in high esteem)

*Nha Pincha:* Let's push. (an expression used during the struggle for independence)

*pano de terra*: a special cloth worn around a woman's waist

*porginha*: a type of bean with many uses

Nha
Pincha